W9-BSY-375

The Living
OCEAN

Robert A. Mattson

The Living World Series

ENSLOW PUBLISHERS, INC.

Bloy St. & Ramsey Ave.	Box 38
Box 777	Aldershot
Hillside, N.J. 07205	Hants GU12 6BP
U.S.A.	U.K.

Juv. QH541.14.M38 1991+

Copyright © 1991 by Robert A. Mattson

All rights reserved.

No part of this book may be reproduced by any means without the written
permission of the publisher.

Library of Congress Cataloging-in-Publication Data:

Mattson, Robert A.
    The Living Ocean / Robert A. Mattson.
      p. cm. — (The living world series)
    Summary: Explores the ocean environment as a habitat for life, the kinds of
organisms found in the ocean, and the relations of people to the sea.
    ISBN 0-89490-277-6
    1. Marine ecology—Juvenile literature. 2. Seafaring life—
Juvenile literature.   [1. Marine ecology. 2. Ocean. 3. Ecology.]
    I. Title. II. Series.
    QH541.14.M38 1991
    574.5'2636—dc20   89-25791
                                          CIP
                                          AC

Printed in the United States of America

10 9 8 7 6 5 4 3 2 1

Illustration Credits:
Mike Bacon, 37, 39; Pat Batchelder, 7, 13, 24, 30; Department of Natural Resources,
Florida Marine Research Institute, 18; J. Frederick Grassle; Woods Hole
Oceanographic Institution, 47; R. Lewis; Mangrove Systems, Inc., 50; L.P. Madin;
Woods Hole Oceanographic Institution, 19; Robert A. Mattson, 4, 6, 9, 18, 19, 31,
38, 43, 45, 54; Berry Shafii, 21, 35, 46, 55.

Cover Photo: Robert A. Mattson

Contents

Waves breaking on a shoreline.

1/The Marine Environment

On the West Coast of Florida is a large estuary called Tampa Bay. Early explorers were amazed by the richness of its marine life. In 1883, a sportsman wrote about his trip to the bay:

"....about three o'clock (we) pulled up and went home, well satisfied with our day's work. We had over a hundred pounds of fish, including....drum, sheephead, grunters and seatrout. I shall never forget this day's sport, no matter what other rich or varied sports I may enjoy in the future, so great was the variety of fish caught and so exciting the nature of the fishing." (FROM: Rustling in the Rockies: Hunting and Fishing by Mountain and Stream, by G. O. Shields)

"Old-timers" who have lived near the bay for many years talk about the large numbers of fish and other marine life the bay used to contain. Today, most of Tampa Bay is surrounded by the bustling cities of Tampa and St. Petersburg. Many areas of the bay are no longer good fishing areas, and some areas are not even safe for swimming. This story is the same for many bays and estuaries throughout the world.

5

What caused these changes? How could they have been prevented?

This story shows why it is important to study the ocean biome and why it is necessary to understand its ecology. Ecology is the branch of biology that studies the interaction of living organisms with their environment and with one another. Ecologists study different biomes to understand how they are organized and how they work, which includes studying and understanding the effects of humans on a biome. It is important to understand the ecology of a biome in order to preserve the resources people find desirable such as abundant fish or clean water.

THE OCEANS

There are four major world oceans: the Pacific Ocean, the Atlantic Ocean, the Indian Ocean, and the Arctic Ocean. Together, they cover 71 percent of the earth's surface. The Pacific Ocean is the largest.

Within the basins of each of these oceans are certain kinds of geological features: the continental shelf, continental slope, abyssal

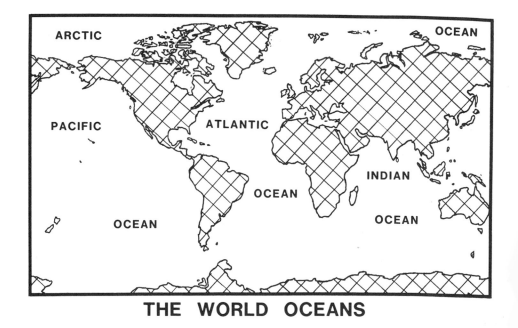

THE WORLD OCEANS

6

plains, oceanic ridges, trenches, and seamounts. These geological seafloor features can be found in all of the major world oceans. It is important to know about them because different types of animals and plants are found living in, on, and around each feature.

Along the coasts of the continents, certain kinds of geographic areas are found where the ocean meets the land. Bays, lagoons, and sounds are bodies of water partly or mostly surrounded by land and connected to the ocean. Examples are: Chesapeake Bay, Long Island Sound, and the Indian River lagoon, on the East Coast of the United States.

Lagoons and bays may be found behind barrier islands. These are coastal islands formed by the action of waves and currents. Along the East Coast of the United States are systems of barrier islands with lagoons or bays behind them. Examples are the barrier islands at Cape

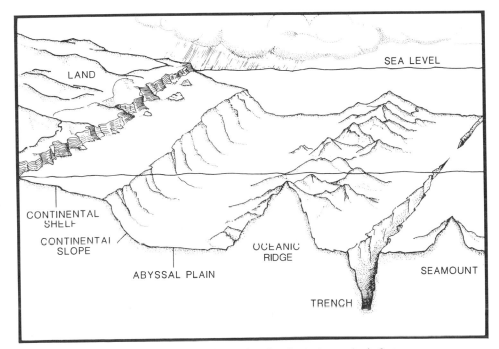

Cross section of the ocean floor, showing the major geologic features.

Kennedy, Florida, and Cape Hatteras, North Carolina. Passes or inlets are the connections between lagoons or bays and the open ocean. An estuary is an area where freshwater from a river or stream mixes with seawater.

WHAT IS SEAWATER?

Salinity

Seawater contains salt. Most of these salts came from the land after the oceans were formed millions of years ago. The major salt in seawater is sodium chloride, the same salt as table salt. There are other types of chemical compounds called "salts" in seawater. These are presented in the following table:

SALT	CHEMICAL SYMBOL	PERCENT COMPOSITION
sodium chloride	$NaCl$	66.7 %
magnesium chloride	$MgCl$	14.5 %
sodium sulfate	Na_3SO_4	11.6 %
calcium chloride	$CaCl_2$	2.9 %
potassium chloride	KCl_2	2.0 %
other compounds	—	2.3 %

Salinity is the term used to describe the total amount of salt present in seawater. It is measured in "parts per thousand" (abbreviated ‰). The Atlantic Ocean is the saltiest of the major world oceans, with an average salinity of 36‰.

Salinity is important because some marine organisms only tolerate water at a specific salinity, while others tolerate a broad range of salinity. Salinity is an environmental condition which determines where different kinds of organisms can live in the ocean. Salinity is also important because one of the salts found in seawater contains calcium. Calcium is used by many marine organisms to build their shells and skeletons.

Temperature

Energy from the sun shines on the earth and warms the atmosphere and the oceans. The amount of heat energy contained in the air or water is expressed as the temperature. Temperature can be measured using either the Fahrenheit scale ("degrees F," or ° F) or the Celsius scale ("degrees C," or ° C). Scientists usually use the Celsius scale. On this scale, water freezes at 0° C (32° F) and boils at 100° C (212° F).

The sun shines most intensely, and for the longest amount of time during the year, on the regions of the world around the equator. It shines the least at the poles. This is one reason why there are warmer areas of the ocean and cooler areas. Certain types of organisms only live in warm-water areas, while others only live in cold water areas. Based on the average year-round water temperature, the world's oceans are divided into five major regions: polar regions (cold areas), subpolar regions (moderately cold areas), temperate regions (moderate areas), subtropical regions (moderately warm areas), and tropical regions (warm areas).

Ocean temperatures not only vary in different parts of the world, they also vary with the depth of the water. The deeper areas of the ocean are colder. In all of the world's oceans below a depth of 6,600

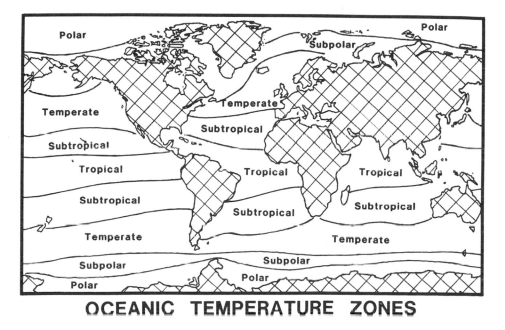

OCEANIC TEMPERATURE ZONES

to 9,900 feet (2,000 to 3,000 meters), the temperature never rises above 4° C (39° F).

In some locations in the ocean, the water is well mixed from top to bottom, and the water temperature decreases gradually with depth. In other locations, a layer of warm water is found at the surface over a layer of cold water at the bottom. The water temperature changes suddenly at the boundary between these two layers of water. This boundary, or zone, is called a thermocline. It can act as a barrier, blocking the movement of gases, food material, and even organisms between the surface and bottom layers.

Gases and Nutrients

Animals and plants require oxygen (O_2) to live. Plants also require carbon dioxide (CO_2) to produce food. Both of these gases are found dissolved in seawater. The amounts dissolved depend on the temperature and salinity of the water. Cold water holds more gas than warm water, and salt water holds less gas than freshwater.

There is usually enough CO_2 in seawater to support plant life. The amount of O_2 dissolved in seawater, however, can change very much, and can determine whether or not organisms can live in an area. Locations with enough oxygen to support life are called aerobic environments. Most marine organisms require an aerobic environment. Locations with very little or no oxygen are called anaerobic environments. There are few organisms that can tolerate anaerobic conditions.

Marine plants also require nutrients (certain kinds of chemicals) to help them manufacture their food materials from CO_2, water, and sunlight (the process known as photosynthesis). Two important plant nutrients found in seawater are nitrogen and phosphorous.

Sometimes, a location in the ocean may have large amounts of one or more of these nutrients in the water. These nutrient-rich locations are called eutrophic areas. Some locations are naturally eutrophic, such as upwelling areas. Things people do, such as dumping sewage into the ocean, can also create eutrophic areas. By affecting the amounts of nutrients in seawater, people can affect the kinds of marine organisms that live in a particular location.

WHAT ARE TIDES, WAVES AND CURRENTS?

Tides

Tides are the periodic rise and fall of the level of the ocean each day caused by the gravitational pull of the sun and the moon. Even though the sun is many times bigger than the moon, the moon is closer to the earth. Because of this, its gravitational pull is stronger than that of the sun and is more important in determining the tides.

The gravitational pull of the moon on the oceans is strong enough to change their level. As the earth rotates each day, a particular location on the earth moves through areas where the pull of the moon is stronger. Here, the water will be deeper due to this pull (a high tide). This location also passes through areas where the pull is weaker. Here the water will be shallower (a low tide).

Many parts of the world experience two high and two low tides each day. Other parts of the world experience one high and one low tide each day, and still other locations have a mixed cycle of tides, sometimes two high and two low tides, sometimes only one of each. This is caused by the shapes of the ocean basins and the presence and depth of underwater features such as continental shelves.

The gravitational pull of the sun has some influence on the tide cycle. For a few days, twice each month, the pull of the sun and moon are in line (during the full and new phases of the moon), and a location will experience higher high tides and lower low tides at this time. These are called the spring tides (though they occur throughout the year, not just in the spring). For a few days at two other times during each month (the quarter phases of the moon), the sun and moon pull at right angles. The high tides are not quite as high and the low tides not quite as low as usual. These are called neap tides.

Because of the tides, the water level changes each day on a

shoreline. This creates several zones on the shore. The intertidal zone is the area of shoreline between the high and low tide levels; it is underwater at high tide and exposed to the air at low tide. Shoreline areas above the highest high tide are in the splash zone (called this because these areas get wet only by splashing from waves). Shoreline areas below the level of the lowest low tide are in the subtidal zones. These areas are usually underwater.

Certain organisms are adapted to survive in each of these tide zones, based partly on their ability to tolerate drying out at low tide. Some organisms are only active at high tide, others are only active at low tide. The tide acts as a kind of "clock"; it regulates the behavior of shoreline organisms.

Waves

Waves in the ocean are caused by the wind. As the wind blows, it "drags" against the surface of the water, creating waves. You can duplicate this in miniature by taking a shallow pan or bowl of water and blowing gently across the surface of the water. The small ripples you see are miniature waves. The distance the wind blows over the surface of the water is called the fetch. The longer the fetch, the larger the waves produced will be. Larger waves are also produced by winds that blow stronger, or by those that blow for a longer period of time.

As waves are generated by the wind, they move through the water. As a wave moves closer to the shore, the water depth below the wave decreases. When the depth of the water is about one-half the wavelength (the distance from wave crest to wave crest), the wave gets higher and steeper. As the wave moves into even shallower water, it topples over and "breaks," causing the foaming waves we see at the beach. The breaking of waves on the shoreline can have much power. This affects the animals and plants living there.

Currents and Upwelling

Currents are the horizontal movement of water in the ocean from one location to another. There are several kinds of currents, each produced in a different way.

12

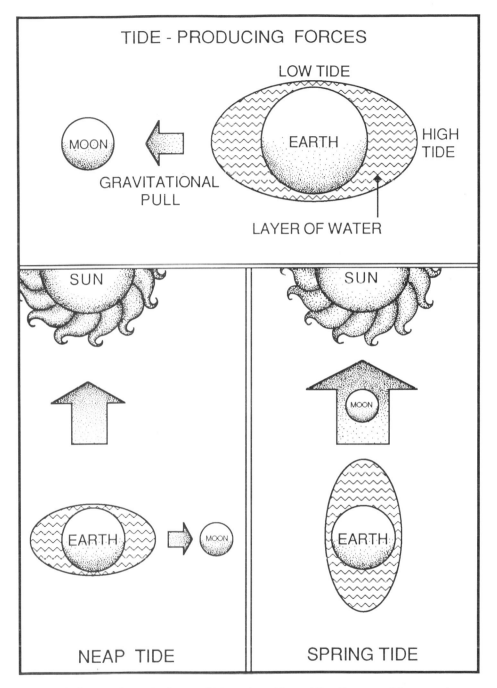

This diagram shows the forces which produce tides and the alignment of the sun and moon during spring and neap tides.

Large surface currents present in the oceans (such as the Gulf Stream and the Equatorial Current) are produced by winds (such as the trade winds) that regularly blow over the surface of the ocean. These large ocean currents are important influences on the climate of the continents, and are also important in helping marine organisms travel from one area to another.

Other types of currents are tidal currents. These are produced by the movement of water due to the rise and fall of the tide. Where water is moving through a pass or inlet, very strong tidal currents called rip currents can be produced. Longshore currents are another type of current found near the coast. These are currents which move along the shoreline parallel to the shore itself. Longshore currents are important in moving sand along coastlines and helping to maintain beaches and barrier islands.

Water can move vertically in the ocean as well as horizontally. This vertical movement of water from the ocean bottom is called upwelling. It is important because it transports food and nutrients from deeper parts of the ocean, where they are unavailable to plants and animals, to the surface where they can be used.

2/Ecology of Marine Plants and Animals

The branch of biology that is concerned with naming, describing, and classifying living organisms is called taxonomy. The standard way of naming living things in biology is with the system of binomial nomenclature (which means "two-word name"). With this scientific naming system, scientists throughout the world can name organisms in a language they all understand. The particular language used to name living things is Latin. The scientific name is always italicized or underlined because it is in a language that is different from the other words on the printed page.

All living organisms that are known have been given a two-word scientific name. The first word is the genus name. It is somewhat like a last name (even though it comes first), in that it tells generally what the organism is and what other organisms it is closely related to (just as your last name tells that you are closely related to your family members). The second word in the scientific name is the species name. It tells specifically what the organism is (just as your first name tells specifically who you are).

15

WHAT DO MARINE ECOLOGISTS STUDY?

Marine scientists who study the ecology of the oceans usually study populations and communities of marine organisms. Populations are groups of individuals of the same species, such as a population of common dolphins or a population of blue crabs. Communities are groups of populations of different organisms found in a given place. Examples are kelp communities found along parts of the California coast and salt marsh communities in Chesapeake Bay.

Within a community, each organism has a niche, a particular position that the organism occupies in nature. The niche of an organism includes what it eats, what eats it, and where it lives. Where an organism lives is partly determined by its ability to tolerate the salinity, temperature, and oxygen content of the water. Therefore, environmental conditions such as these help define the niche of an organism.

The habitat of an organism is the specific area in a community where it prefers to live. For example, a species of mud crab that lives in salt marshes prefers the habitat found in the mussel and oyster beds within the marsh community. The concepts of niche and habitat are important because if people change or modify a marine community so that certain habitats are destroyed, or the temperature or salinity are changed, organisms that depend upon those conditions won't be able to survive.

Two parts of the environment are important in determining whether or not organisms may live within a community; physical conditions and biological conditions. These two types of environmental conditions act to organize communities in the marine biome. They determine what organisms live in a community, how many live there, and where they are found.

Physical conditions include many of the things discussed in Chapter 1: salinity, temperature, wave action, etc. As mentioned before, each organism tolerates a certain range of each of these conditions. If people change the temperature or salinity of the environment, they can kill certain species of organisms that cannot tolerate the new conditions.

Biological conditions include the types of habitat present and the interactions of organisms in a community with each other. The two main types of interactions are competition and predation.

Competition occurs when two organisms have similar niches. The organism that is the better competitor will usually be found in the community, either by itself or in much greater numbers than the organism that is the poorer competitor.

Predation occurs when one organism (the predator) eats another (the prey) for food. Predation can limit the numbers of organisms that may occur in a habitat, or may even exclude certain types of organisms from a particular habitat. Examples of predation and competition will be discussed in the following chapters.

In addition to competition, predation, habitat, and physical factors, the ability to move from one area to another by dispersal may determine where organisms are found. Those with good dispersal ability are found in many types of communities. Those with poor dispersal ability are found only in specific communities.

HOW DO MARINE ECOLOGISTS DESCRIBE MARINE ORGANISMS?

By Size: Microscopic and Macroscopic

One way of describing a particular animal or plant is according to how large it is. Organisms that require some type of instrument in order to see them are microscopic organisms. Organisms that can be clearly seen with the naked eye are called macroscopic.

Microscopic plants in the ocean include many types of small plants called phytoplankton. Diatoms and dinoflagellates are two examples. Macroscopic marine plants include large algae (such as kelp and sea lettuce), underwater seagrasses, and salt marsh grasses.

Microscopic animals include many types of zooplankton. Copepods, tiny jellyfish, and the larvae (the young) of many larger marine animals are all zooplankton. Macroscopic animals include fish, shrimp, crabs, and whales.

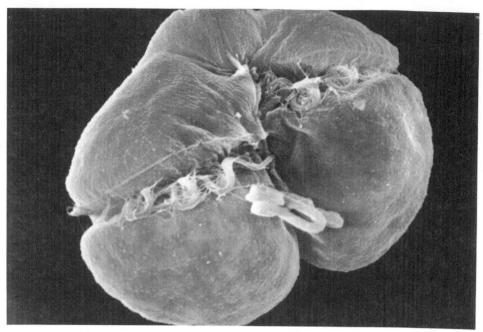

A scanning electron microscope photograph of a marine dinoflagellate, an example of a microscopic plant.

A salt marsh. Several examples of macroscopic plants are found here, such as grasses and rushes.

A photomicrograph of a copepod, an example of a microscopic marine animal.

Photograph of fiddler crabs in a coastal marsh. The male crabs have a greatly enlarged claw. Crabs are macroscopic animals

By Where It Lives: Benthic and Pelagic

One of the main ways marine ecologists describe marine plants and animals is based on where they are found living in the ocean. Organisms that live on or within the bottom of the ocean are called benthic organisms. Those that float or swim in the water are pelagic organisms.

Benthic animals living on the surface of the bottom attached to rock or living on the surface of the sediment are called epifauna. Those that live buried in the sediment are called infauna.

Plankton are microscopic, pelagic organisms that include planktonic plants (phytoplankton) and planktonic animals (zooplankton). The word plankton comes from the Greek word for "wanderer," which describes the plankton well. Most are at the mercy of currents, drifting about with little ability to swim for long distances.

Nekton are larger pelagic organisms that have good swimming ability. Nekton include most larger, familiar animals such as fish, whales, and squid. Note that some animals, particularly many invertebrates, begin life as microscopic planktonic larvae. As they grow, they become part of the nekton or the benthic fauna.

By What It Eats: Food Webs

Another way to describe marine organisms is based on their position in the food web. In all natural communities of organisms, there exists a "web of life" based on how an organism obtains its food. Most food webs start with plants. Plants are autotrophic organisms (which means "self-feeding"). Plants produce their own food through the process of photosynthesis. Because of this, plants are called primary producers. Animals are heterotrophic organisms, meaning they cannot produce their own food. Herbivores are animals which obtain food by eating plants. Carnivores are organisms which obtain food by eating animals.

A third major group of organisms in food webs are the decomposers. These include plant-like organisms called bacteria and fungi. Most of these are heterotrophic, obtaining nutrition by breaking down dead plants and animals. By doing this, they perform the important job of releasing the nutrients and other substances contained in the dead organisms. These materials are then available for recycling.

On land, much of the living material produced by plants may be consumed directly as green leaves or twigs. In the ocean biome, few animals eat the green leaves or other living parts of plants. Most living plant material dies and falls off the plant. Bacteria and fungi (the decomposers) then begin to grow on the dead plant material. Many small marine animals use this material with its attached decomposers as food. The bits of decaying plant material are called detritus.

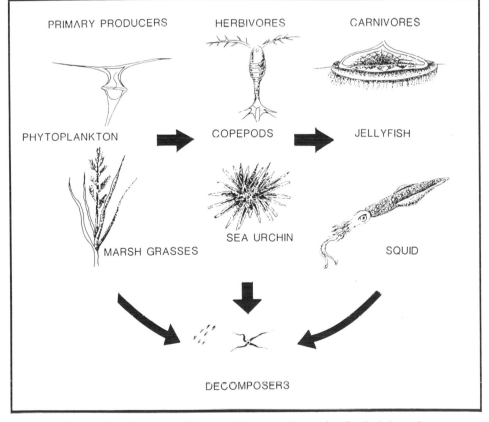

A diagram showing some of the typical parts of a marine food chain; primary producers, herbivores, carnivores, and decomposers.

3/Ecology of the Coastal Areas

The coast is the place where the sea meets the land. Coastal areas include portions of the continental shelf near the actual shoreline. Many kinds of marine organisms are found in coastal areas. They all have ways to survive in the changing, sometimes harsh conditions present in the coastal areas.

Most of the food harvested from the sea by humans comes from coastal areas. Some areas of the coast have been badly damaged by the activities of humans. Because of these two facts, a lot of scientific research has been done on coastal marine communities in the ocean. Yet, there is much more that needs to be learned. It is important to have an understanding of coastal ecology if our coasts are to be protected from more damage by human activities.

ROCKY COASTS

On most rocky coastlines, distinct color bands (some white, some black, some brownish-green) are seen when the rocks are exposed at low tide. Each of these bands represents a particular zone where certain kinds of animals and plants live.

The uppermost zone on the rocks, in the splash zone, usually has a black color. This is due to the presence of two types of microscopic organisms living on the rocks called blue-green algae and lichens. Small snails called periwinkles also live in the splash zone. These snails feed on the algae and lichens by scraping them off the rocks.

Periwinkles are found on almost every rocky shore throughout the world. Some live in the splash zone and others live in parts of the intertidal zone. Those living in the splash zone are able to live above the high tide line, away from the water, for long periods of time. They carry water with them in their shell, and use it to keep their gills moist. They return to the water to lay their eggs or to renew their water supply.

The next color zone, the intertidal zone, is often white. This is due to the presence of barnacles. These small animals are crustaceans (related to shrimp and crabs). Each individual barnacle produces a cone-shaped shell around itself, made of several plates. Barnacles attach to the rocks using a powerful glue. This glue and the cone shape

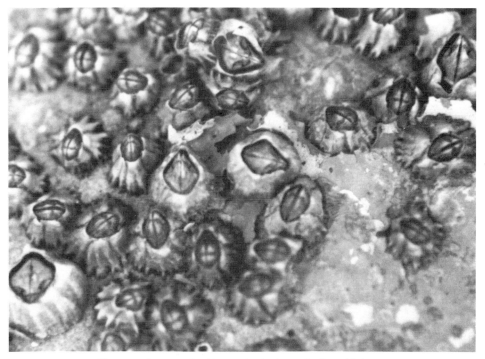

Close up photograph of barnacles in the rocky intertidal zone

of the shell enable the barnacles to stay attached to the rocks and resist being knocked off by the force of the waves pounding on them.

Below the zone of barnacles, or sometimes intermingled with them, is a bluish-black colored zone of mussels. These animals are bivalve molluscs (related to clams and scallops). Like the barnacles, they have ways to resist the force of the waves pounding the rocky shoreline. They attach themselves to the rocks using a clump of strong threads called a byssus. This byssus and their wedge-like shape help them resist the force of the waves.

Barnacles and mussels feed on plankton at high tide (when they are covered with water). The mussels filter water through their gills to trap plankton. Barnacles sweep the water with their appendages (legs) to trap plankton. Barnacles and mussels close their shells at low tide, trapping water inside, in order to survive until the next high tide covers them.

In the lower intertidal and subtidal zones, a brown or green zone dominated by some type of algae is usually found. Algae are plants which do not bear flowers or seeds and which do not have true leaves, stems or roots. Algae attach themselves to the rocks using a specialized structure called a holdfast. Most algae do not tolerate drying out, and so they are found in subtidal areas, where they are wet most of the time. Kelp forests are a particular type of community of large

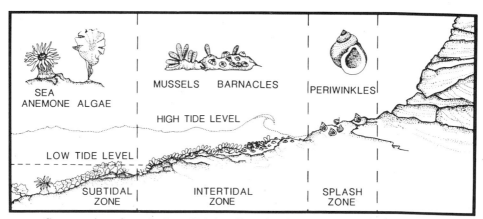

Cross-section of a rocky intertidal shoreline, showing the zonation exhibited by the organisms. Examples are shown of typical rocky intertidal organisms.

24

marine algae found living in the subtidal zone on some coasts.

On the rocky coast, the pattern of zonation is produced by the two types of environmental conditions discussed earlier: physical and biological conditions. At low tide, the intertidal zone is exposed to the air. Organisms that can tolerate a longer time of exposure to the air will be able to live where they are exposed to the air more often and longer at low tide. Organisms less tolerant of exposure to air live in the lower intertidal or the subtidal zone, where they are infrequently or never exposed. This is an example of how physical conditions, such as the tide, limit the zone of the shoreline that organisms can live in.

The different species on a rocky shore also interact with one another. Competition occurs when two species of organisms try to use the same resource or, as ecologists say, occupy similar niches. Living space for attachment is an important resource on the rocky coast. Scientists have shown that two species of barnacle (species "B" and species "C") compete for space in the rocky intertidal zone. C occurs only in the upper half of the barnacle zone, while B occurs in the lower half of the barnacle zone. Barnacle C can live lower in the intertidal zone, but it normally is not found there because B crowds it out. This is an example of how competition can influence the zonation of organisms on the shore.

Predation is also important in determining where organisms live on the rocky shore. Mussels are able to outcompete barnacles for space in the intertidal zone, so that what might start out as a mixed mussel and barnacle zone will eventually become a pure mussel zone with no barnacles. However, on some rocky shores on the coast of the northwestern United States, a mixture of mussels and barnacles may be found. What prevents the mussels from excluding the barnacles from the community?

Experiments showed that individuals of a species of sea star, called *Pisaster ochreaus*, move up into the mussel/barnacle zone at high tide to feed on the mussels. At low tide, the star retreats to the algae zone to await the next high tide. By feeding on the mussels (an example of predation), the sea stars control the mussel population on

25

the shore. This prevents mussels from dominating the barnacles.

The sea star in this example is called a keystone species, because if it is removed, the whole community changes. The community would become dominated by mussels, and animals which depend on barnacles for food or habitat would no longer be able to live there. This example shows how predation is an important biological condition on the rocky shore.

SANDY COASTS

On rocky coastlines, the communities of organisms are easily visible, and the patterns of zonation are clearly seen. Zonation is present on sandy coasts as well, but it is not always visible because most of the animals live under the surface of the sediment (the soft sand or mud). Few animals live on the sediment surface, because it is easily shifted about by waves. Particular types of communities of plants are found growing on some sandy coasts.

There are basically two types of sandy coastlines; high-wave-energy beaches and low-wave-energy beaches. Each type of sandy coast supports different communities of animals and plants. This is due to differences in the size and strength of the waves that occur on each type of coast and variations in the kinds of sediments on each beach.

High Wave-Energy Beaches

High energy beaches are usually found on coasts facing the open sea such as those on the East Coast of the United States, facing the Atlantic Ocean. On these coasts, large heavy waves regularly pound the shore. High energy beaches usually occur where there is a large fetch to create the large waves. Sediments of high-energy beaches are usually course sand or pebbles.

A typical feature of high-energy beaches are sand dunes. Sand dunes are formed by the action of wind. Certain types of grasses (such as sea oats and maram grass) grow on the dunes and accumulate more sand by trapping it among their roots and stems. These grasses are important in helping to maintain the dunes.

Sand dunes are important because they serve as a reservoir of sand which helps to maintain the sandy beach. They also protect the beach during severe storms with very large waves, and they provide habitat for many animals.

The sand dunes are an important part of the beach ecology, but they can be easily damaged by the activities of people. Some people build their homes on dunes so they can get a nice view of the ocean. Others race over dunes in dune buggies and all-terrain vehicles. These kinds of activities destroy dune habitats and harm the entire beach.

In the intertidal zone of high energy beaches, animals that live buried in the sand have ways to rebury themselves rapidly if uncovered by a heavy wave. Examples of these are the mole crab and the coquina (or donax) clam. These animals, like the barnacles and mussels of the rocky coast, feed on plankton during high tide.

Sea oats growing on a sand dune on a high energy sandy shoreline. These grasses help stabilize the dunes and provide habitat for animals which live on the dunes.

In the subtidal areas of these coasts live larger animals such as razor clams, venus clams, moon snails, and crabs. Crabs and snails (such as whelks) move into the intertidal zone at high tide to feed on the small animals in the sand. At low tide shorebirds, such as sandpipers and willets, probe the sand for small infauna to eat. Few species of plants are able to grow in the intertidal and subtidal zones of high-energy coastlines because of the strong waves.

Low-Wave-Energy Coastlines

Low-energy sandy beaches are found in sheltered locations such as bays, sounds, and estuaries. On these coasts the waves are usually not as large and powerful as those that occur on high energy coasts. Usually, the sediments on these shores are finer and muddier. Sand dunes are usually not found on low-energy sandy beaches because these beaches don't have the strong winds that form and shape sand dunes.

One group of animals which is very common in the infauna of these coasts are polychaete worms. Many different species of these annelids (related to the earthworm) live on these shorelines. The plumed worm is a polychaete that constructs a tube, most of which lies buried, with the tip projecting above the surface of the sediment. The worm cements bits of seaweed or shell to the tip of the tube. These worms usually live in the intertidal zone in groups called worm beds.

A few animals are able to exist as epifauna (on the surface of the sediment) in the intertidal zone of low-energy beaches. The nassa mud snails are small snails (0.5 inch, or 1.3 cm long) usually found crawling on the surface of the sediment. They feed on bits of dead animal and plant material and on microscopic organisms living in the sediment.

More species of polychaetes live in the subtidal zone of low-energy beaches. Examples are the lugworm, the bamboo worm, and the bristle worm. Many of these polychaetes eat the sediment itself and digest the small particles of food in it. Animals that feed this way are called deposit feeders. Some polychaetes use sand grains to build tubes to live in. Clams such as razor clams and tellins also live in the subtidal zone of low-energy beaches.

The sediments of the subtidal zone are sometimes very anaerobic. Many of the animals that live deep within these sediments have burrows or tubes to the surface, which enable them to pump oxygen-rich water down to themselves at high tide.

Plants of Low-Energy Sandy Coasts

Some species of plants are able to grow on low-energy coasts. In some areas salt marshes are found. These are communities of marsh grasses and rushes adapted to living in the intertidal zone. Many different species of animals are found in and near the salt marshes. Examples are the ribbed mussel (related to the blue mussels of rocky shores) and fiddler crabs. These small crabs, which live in burrows that they dig, are so named because of the over-sized claw possessed by the male crab. The males use this claw to attract the female crabs and to claim the territory around their burrow.

In subtidal areas, communities of submerged seagrasses may be found. Seagrasses are more complex than the algae of rocky shores. They have true roots, stems and leaves and they bear flowers and seeds. Many species of animals are found living in seagrass beds, such as grass shrimp, pipe fish, seahorses, and brittle stars.

Salt marshes and seagrass beds are coastal wetlands. Many of these wetlands serve as "nurseries" for the young of many larger coastal organisms caught by people for food. The marshes and grass beds provide food and protection from predators for young fish and other small marine animals. These are some of the reasons why coastal wetlands are valuable to humans and why they are protected by laws in many places.

People once regarded salt marshes, seagrass beds and other types of coastal wetlands as "wasteland." These were the areas that were frequently dredged and filled to create waterfront property for houses and marinas. The efforts of many scientists have now shown that these coastal wetlands are vital for many of the species of fish, crabs, and shrimp that people harvest for food.

Zonation on Sandy Coasts

The animals and plants living on sandy coastlines do exhibit zonation; that is, different groups of organisms are found in the intertidal and subtidal zones. As on the rocky coasts, this is due to both physical and biological conditions.

In salt marshes, different zones of plants can be seen. This plant zonation is mainly due to the tolerance each type of plant has to being flooded by high tide. Cordgrass usually occurs closest to the water in the intertidal zone because it is able to tolerate more flooding. Seagrasses only occur in the subtidal zone because they cannot tolerate drying out.

Many infauna have to pump water down into their burrow at high tide to obtain food and oxygen. At low tide, they close the burrow and remain inactive until the next high tide. Those unable to tolerate this for a long time will be found in the subtidal zone. Some animals, such as the mole crab of the high energy beaches, require the action of the

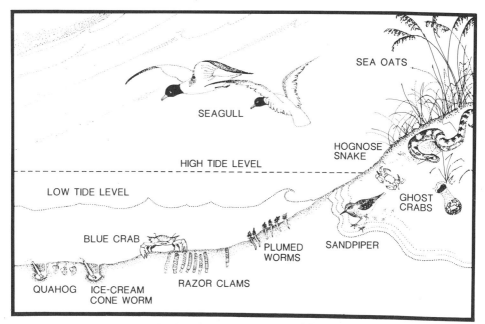

Cross-section of a sandy shoreline, showing some of the organisms which may be found there. Note that this drawing is a combination of both low-wave-energy and high-wave-energy sandy shorelines.

waves (a physical condition) to help them catch plankton, and so these crabs are only found in the intertidal zone, where they are washed by the waves every day.

Another physical condition causing zonation is the type of sediment found at a beach. Deposit feeding polychaetes prefer finer, mud-like sediments, which tend to contain more food material than courser, sandy sediments. More of these worms live in areas of the beach with finer sediments.

A biological factor causing zonation on sandy shores is predation. Predation by crabs on many types of small infauna is prevented by the tubes of the plumed worm. More of these small animals are found in the intertidal zone in the beds of this worm, rather than in bare subtidal areas.

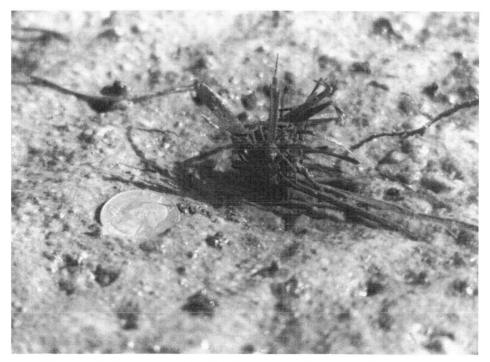

Close-up of a plumed-worm tube. Note how the worm has cemented bits of seaweed to its tube. The coin is a quarter.

4/Ecology of the Offshore Areas

Offshore areas are the open ocean. In coastal areas, both phytoplankton and the plants of the coastal marshes and seagrass beds are the beginning of the food web. In offshore areas, the food web begins with phytoplankton alone. Because of this, the surface areas of the open ocean, where light penetrates the water, are usually the most food-rich areas, and many organisms are found living there. The light is needed by the phytoplankton for their survival. The animals living in the offshore areas have ways to enable them to remain in the food-rich, sunlit, upper parts of the open ocean.

Most of the ocean biome is the open ocean environment. There is much we still must learn about this environment. Some offshore areas may be able to provide much food, minerals, or other natural resources to humans. But, we must have a better understanding of the ecology of these areas if we are to avoid damaging them by our activities.

THE PLANKTON

Phytoplankton

Phytoplankton are the microscopic algae that form the beginning of the food web in the open ocean. The two largest groups of phytoplankton are diatoms and dinoflagellates.

Diatoms are microscopic, single-celled plants or loose colonies of cells. They are found in oceans throughout the world. Diatoms have a cell wall made of silica, which is similar to glass. The different species of diatoms are identified by the shape and pattern of the silica cell wall, called a frustule.

Dinoflagellates are the other major group of phytoplankton. These plants are also single-celled and microscopic. Most have whip-like structures called flagella. The beating of the flagella enables them to move about a little bit. Dinoflagellates tend to be more common in tropical and subtropical waters, while diatoms tend to be more common in temperate and subpolar waters.

Because phytoplankton require light for photosynthesis, they have ways to keep themselves in the upper layers of the open ocean where sunlight penetrates. Their small size is one way; this causes them to sink slowly and remain within the sunlit region of the ocean. Another way is the extensions of the cell wall such as horns, spines, and filaments that many phytoplankton have. These extensions slow the rate of sinking by increasing the surface area of the cell, just as the surface area of a parachute slows the descent of a skydiver to the ground. A third way is the oil droplets some diatoms produce within the cell. Since oil floats on water, these droplets buoy the algal cell, keeping it within the sunlit zone. Oil droplets also serve as a food storage reserve.

In addition to the need for light, phytoplankton require nutrients for growth. When animals and plants living in the water die, they settle to the bottom and are broken down by decomposers. Because of this, nutrients accumulate on the bottom. When the water is well mixed, nutrients that have accumulated on the bottom are brought to the surface water layers, where they are used by phytoplankton for growth.

In polar, subpolar, and temperate areas, the water is well mixed during at least some part of the year. This allows nutrients from the bottom to be brought to the surface where they are used by phytoplankton. In tropical areas, the abundant sunshine always keeps the upper layers of water warm. This establishes a permanent thermocline. This thermocline prevents complete mixing of the water, traps nutrients on the bottom, and does not allow them to be brought back to the surface. The phytoplankton in the upper layers of water use up all the available nutrients.

Zooplankton

Zooplankton are the microscopic animals found in the plankton. Many species of zooplankton feed on the phytoplankton. These herbivorous zooplankton, in turn, are fed upon by larger, carnivorous zooplankton and by small fish. The small fish are eaten by bigger fish. In this way, the zooplankton are the connecting link between the primary producers (the phytoplankton) and the larger, more familiar marine animals. Some species of zooplankton spend their entire lives as plankton, while others only spend part of their lives in the plankton as larvae.

One of the largest groups of zooplankton are the copepods. These are small crustaceans found in ocean waters throughout the world. Most create small currents of water with their appendages and filter phytoplankton out of the water with their mouthparts. Other copepods are carnivorous, feeding on other zooplankton, and a few species are parasites on larger marine animals.

Another group of zooplankton common in the ocean are the euphausiids. Most euphausiids feed on phytoplankton, but a few species are carnivorous. Euphausiids are found throughout the world but tend to be most abundant in polar and subpolar areas. Here, they form dense schools called "krill." These immense swarms of krill are the principal food of the large baleen whales, which strain the krill from the water.

There are many other types of zooplankton found in different regions of the world's oceans. Small planktonic snails called pteropods, predatory arrow worms (called chaetognaths), and small jellyfish live in the zooplankton. Some zooplankton are luminous; they produce light. At night, they create unusual and spectacular displays of natural fireworks in the waters of the ocean.

Other members of the zooplankton are the larvae of larger marine organisms. A planktonic larva enables many benthic animals to disperse to new areas, not by moving there themselves, but by sending their young out into the water. Currents carry the larvae to new locations, where they settle out of the water and grow to adulthood. Many marine invertebrates produce planktonic larvae. A few species of fish (such as plaice) produce planktonic larvae. Many of these animals produce huge numbers of larvae, of which very few survive to adulthood.

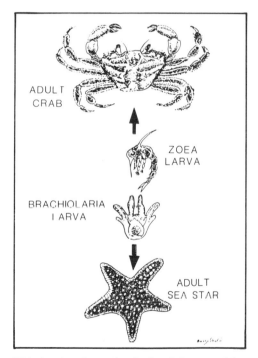

ADULT CRAB

ZOEA LARVA

BRACHIOLARIA LARVA

ADULT SEA STAR

This drawing shows the planktonic larvae and the benthic adults of two typical marine animals.

Like the phytoplankton, many species of zooplankton have spines, horns, and other extensions of the body that increase their surface area, enabling them to stay in the upper areas of the ocean where phytoplankton are plentiful. These spines also serve as a defense against predators by making the zooplankton difficult to swallow.

Some zooplankton move up and down for considerable distances in the water during the day. This is called vertical migration. This ability may help them avoid predators. By going deeper during the day (where it is darker) and coming to the surface at night, they aren't seen as easily by predators. Vertical migration may also enable zooplankton to move into currents present at different depths in the water, allowing them to move to new areas or to remain within a given area.

THE NEKTON

Larger open ocean animals are the nekton. Most nekton are fish and most have good swimming ability. Some of these are fish that feed on plankton, such as anchovies and sardines. These small plankton-eating fish, in turn, are fed upon by larger fish. In areas near the coasts, many fish are caught by people either commercially (for food) or for sport.

Some open ocean fish migrate long distances, in many cases using the large ocean currents to assist them. Many of these larger fish (such as mackerel and tuna) are carnivores, feeding on other fish and squid. They have streamlined body shapes and other features that make them efficient swimmers.

Anadromous fish, such as salmon, live their adult lives in the ocean, but return to freshwater rivers and streams to spawn. The young fish hatch and live for a short period of time in the river, then migrate to the sea to mature and live their adult lives there. Catadromous fish live their adult lives in freshwater, but return to the sea to spawn. The American and European eels are examples of catadromous fish. The long distances traveled by these fish are known to be aided by the large ocean currents.

Invertebrates of the nekton include some species of shrimp,

squids, and cuttlefish. Some species of squid are the largest known living invertebrates, growing to lengths of 56 feet (17 meters). These large squids live in the deep ocean. Squids are mollusks, related to clams and snails. They are all predators, feeding on other invertebrates and fish, using special tentacles for capturing their prey. Some squid gather into large groups called schools.

Other invertebrate members of the nekton have poor swimming ability, but are included in the nekton because of their size. Two of the more common species are open ocean jellyfish called the Portugese man-of-war and the By-the-wind sailor. Both float on the surface, with their tentacles hanging down into the water. They feed on fish and small invertebrates, which are stung and paralyzed by the tentacles when they swim into them. Their float organ possesses a small wing-like "sail" that enables them to take advantage of the wind to move them from place to place.

The largest ocean animals are the most familiar members of the

Underwater photograph of a whaler shark. The shark is an example of nekton.

nekton. These are sharks, sea turtles, a few species of marine birds, and large marine mammals.

Sharks are fish. They use their gills to extract oxygen from the water. Their skeleton is composed of cartilage, not bone. Most are scavengers or predators, feeding on dead or injured fish and other animals. The two largest sharks, however, consume plankton. These are the whale shark (which grows to 50 feet or 15.2 meters) and the basking shark (which grows to 45 feet or 13.6 meters).

Sea turtles are reptiles, related to freshwater turtles, lizards, and snakes. Examples of sea turtles are the loggerhead, green, hawksbill, leatherback, and Atlantic Ridley turtles. They all possess flippers, rather than the webbed feet and legs seen on freshwater turtles. They are air-breathing and are adapted to live their entire lives in the ocean. However, all sea turtles must return to the land to lay their eggs. Eggs are laid in a nest dug by the female on a sandy beach.

Two green turtles (*Chelonia mydas*). These marine turtles live their entire adult life at sea but return to the land to lay their eggs.

Sea turtles feed on seagrasses, other marine plants, and animals. A few sea turtles feed on jellyfish. Unfortunately, these turtles can be killed by eating clear plastic bags that people carelessly throw into the ocean. The turtles mistake the bags for jellyfish.

Marine birds that are considered members of the nekton are some of the "swimming birds". Examples are cormorants, puffins, penguins, grebes, and loons. Some of these birds do not fly well. Penguins cannot fly at all. Their wings and feathers are adapted for swimming.

Examples of marine mammals are whales, dolphins, manatees, seals and walruses. All are air-breathing, warm-blooded mammals that have special adaptations that enable them to dive deep and stay underwater for a long time.

There are two main kinds of whales:

1. Baleen whales. The name comes from the name given to the large plates (baleen) in the mouths of these whales used to strain

Seals on an ice floe in Alaska.

plankton from the water. Examples of baleen whales are the blue, right, humpback, and grey whales.

2. Toothed whales. These whales are all carnivores and predators. Examples are sperm whales (the largest of the toothed whales), orcas (or killer whales), dolphins, and porpoises.

The blue whale, a baleen whale, is the largest animal to have ever lived on the earth—larger even than any of the dinosaurs! Many baleen whales are so large that only by feeding on plankton can they find and eat enough food to live. The largest toothed whale, the sperm whale, feeds on large squid found deep in the ocean. Some older sperm whales have many "sucker scars" on their heads from battles with giant squid.

Whales have poor eyesight. They find food and navigate using sounds that travel through the water and reflect off objects. Their keen hearing allows whales to detect the reflections, which enables them to tell how far away an object is, how big it is, how fast it is moving, and other information.

5/Ecology of the Polar, Tropical, and Deep Ocean Areas

Areas of the ocean with special types of communities of animals and plants not found in most other parts of the world are the polar areas, the tropical areas, and the deep oceans. These marine communities are unique and can be easily damaged by human activities, so it is very important to understand their ecology.

POLAR OCEANS

Polar areas of the ocean are: the arctic regions around the North Pole, and the antarctic regions around the South Pole. The animals and plants living in the oceans in these areas have had to adapt to two related environmental conditions: cold temperatures and ice. Because of the harsh conditions, fewer species of animals and plants are found in the arctic and antarctic areas compared to other areas of the ocean. Those organisms that do live there, however, can be very abundant.

41

To withstand the cold, many cold-blooded animals of polar areas have special chemicals in their blood to prevent their body fluids from freezing, which would kill them. The icefish is an example of this type of animal. The warm-blooded animals (birds and marine mammals) have thick layers of feathers, fur or layers of fat (called blubber) to help insulate them from the cold.

The arctic and antarctic regions of the world do not support the same communities of large polar animals. Penguins are found only in antarctic regions, while walruses are found only in arctic regions. Seals are found at both poles, as are orcas and most whales. Large quantities of plankton are found in the waters of polar seas because these waters naturally contain a lot of nutrients. This is why some of the largest whales (such as the blue whale) are found in polar areas, because only in polar areas is there enough plankton food for them.

The animals and plants living on the shorelines of polar areas have had to adapt to the presence of ice during part or all of the year. Some animals move to deeper waters, underneath the ice, to await the coming of warmer weather when the ice melts. Animals and plants that cannot move (such as barnacles and algae attached to rocks) may be scraped from the shoreline and killed. The areas scraped bare are recolonized after the ice melts by organisms that were living in protected areas.

The air-breathing mammals of the polar seas have also had to adapt to ice. Seals and walruses create holes in the ice to breath through. During times of the year when the surface of the sea is covered with ice, they remain near these breathing holes and keep them open. Some large mammals migrate to warmer areas during polar winters to avoid ice.

Polar and subpolar areas are productive and valuable fishery areas for humans. The nutrient rich waters permit large populations of phytoplankton to build up during the warmer months. The phytoplankton are eaten by zooplankton such as krill, which are eaten by many fish and by baleen whales. Cod, lobster, king crab, and other species are caught in large numbers by commercial fishing fleets from many countries in polar and subpolar regions. Because these areas are such important food-producing areas, it is necessary to protect them from pollution and other damage.

TROPICAL COASTLINES

The warm year-round temperatures of tropical and subtropical areas of the oceans (the regions around the equator) allow many species of animals and plants to live there. Two marine communities found only in tropical and subtropical areas are mangrove swamps and coral reefs.

Mangroves are easily killed by frost and freezing temperatures, so they only grow in subtropical and tropical regions. "Mangrove" refers to species of trees that are able to live in the salty intertidal environment. Mangrove swamps grow on sandy shorelines with low-wave energy.

A mangrove swamp on the west coast of Florida. Note the "prop roots" at the bases of the trees.

The mangrove trees have many features that enable them to survive in their environment. They have a large, shallow root system for support in the soggy sediments of the intertidal zone. The leaves of some mangroves have special glands to secrete excess salt absorbed by the root system.

The seeds of mangrove trees begin to grow before dropping off the parent tree. The young seedlings are carried away by the tide and currents and are washed up on other shores by waves. In this way, the young seedling, since it is growing already, can quickly establish itself on the shoreline.

Many species of animals live in mangrove forests. Some species of crabs are able to climb the trees and feed on the leaves and fruit. Many types of snails, fiddler crabs, and an air-breathing fish, called a mud skipper, live on the forest floor. Species of marine birds, such as cormorant and pelicans, and wading birds (herons and ibis), use mangrove areas for nesting.

Coral reefs are found in subtidal areas on many tropical coastlines. Corals are related to jellyfish and sea anemones, and the actual coral animal is a tiny organism, called a polyp. Many thousands of polyps are joined together to form a coral colony. These colonies extract calcium from the seawater to form the massive stony structures marine ecologists call coral reefs.

Other types of coral, called soft corals, attach to the stony reef. Examples of soft corals are sea fans and sea whips. Soft corals feed mostly on plankton, but many of the large stony coral colonies have algae living within the tissues of the individual coral polyps. The algae survive on nutrients from the coral polyps and the algae, in turn, produce food material for the coral through their photosynthesis.

This relationship is called mutualism. Both the algae and the coral benefit from the relationship. It has been proven by biologists that only corals that contain these algae are able to construct large coral reefs. The algae help the corals to form the reefs by making it easier to extract calcium from the seawater.

Many species of fish are found living around the coral reefs. One type of fish, called a clownfish, lives with certain types of sea anemones on the reef. This is another example of mutualism. The fish lives among the poisonous tentacles of the anemone, but is not harmed by it. In this way, the clownfish is protected from predators among the tentacles. The clownfish lures other fish to the anemone, which kills and eats them. The clownfish feeds on pieces of the prey not eaten by the anemone.

THE DEEP OCEANS

On all the continents, at a depth of about 660 feet (200 meters), the continental shelf slopes sharply downward to a depth of 6,600 to 9,900 feet (2,000 to 3,000 meters), then levels off into the deep ocean bottoms, called the abyssal plains. Eighty-four percent of the ocean bottom is deeper than 6,600 feet (2,000 meters). No sunlight ever penetrates to these depths. The temperature stays at about 39° F (4° C) all the time.

Underwater photograph of a coral reef. The large fish in the center of the photo is a parrotfish. The finger like organisms are soft corals.

One of the most important physical conditions the animals of the deep ocean have had to adapt to is the immense pressure. Most cannot survive when brought up to the surface because the change in pressure is too much and too fast. Because they are so difficult to collect alive, scientists know very little about the life habits of deep ocean animals.

The animals that live on the deep ocean bottom get their food mainly from dead organisms (mostly plankton) that sink down from the surface layers of the water. Many of the organisms that live on the abyssal plains are deposit feeders, eating the sediment and digesting the food material present in it. Examples of deep ocean deposit feeders are sea cucumbers, sea stars, and polychaetes.

Other animals are predators, consuming the other fish and invertebrates that live in the deep ocean. Some of the fish that live here appear to look like creatures from another planet. Some have a tentacle

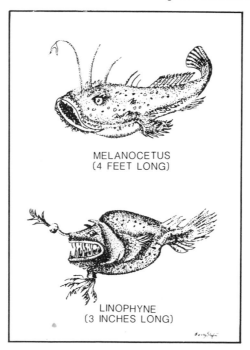

MELANOCETUS
(4 FEET LONG)

LINOPHYNE
(3 INCHES LONG)

Drawings of two fish found in the deep ocean.
The adult length of each is shown under the name
of the animal.

46

or other projection on their body with a small luminous (light producing) organ at the end. They use this as a lure to attract other animals, which they capture for food.

Another habitat in the deep ocean are the trenches. These environments start at a depth of 19,800 feet (6,000 meters). The deepest trenches in the world (for example, the Mariana trench and the Philippine trench) are deeper than 33,000 feet (10,000 meters). Most of the animals found in the trenches are deposit feeders.

An exciting recent discovery in deep ocean ecology was the existence of "thermal rift vent" communities. These are remarkably diverse communities of animals living around hot water springs found in volcanic areas around the mid-oceanic ridges such as near the Galapagos Islands. These spring areas pour out hot water from deep beneath the earth's crust. This hot water contains minerals dissolved from the rock layers of the crust. Bacteria survive on these minerals, and the many types of animals found around the rift vents survive on the bacteria.

Underwater photograph of a thermal rift vent community off the Galapagos Islands. The animals in the tubes are pogonophoran worms. Two crabs are visible on the worm tubes.

A group of worm-like organisms called pogonophorans are abundant around the vents. These large worms live in tubes they build. They have no mouth or gut and obtain nutrition from symbiotic bacteria that live within their tissues. The bacteria survive on the minerals (such as sulfur and iron) in the hot water pouring out of the vents. Crabs, mussels, clams, and fish are also found in these rift vent communities. Some of these also contain symbiotic bacteria that provide food for them.

The deep ocean contains many mysteries that we know little about. In 1938, some fishermen netted an unusual looking fish from deep beneath the Indian Ocean. They had never seen it before, and so they brought it to scientists for identification. The fish was identified to be a coelacanth (SEAL-ah-kanth); a fish that was believed to be extinct for more than 100 million years.

6/Humans and the Oceans

Since early history, people have been interested in the exploration and use of the oceans. The Bible records many examples of use of the sea by people. The Greek philosopher Aristotle was an early marine biologist. During the times of European exploration of the New World, ships were sent out on expeditions to discover and map the coastlines of new territories. The voyages of Columbus, Magellan, and James Cook were early expeditions that provided new knowledge about the oceans. Some of these mapping and surveying expeditions carried aboard a naturalist (a biologist) to collect and record observations on the native plants and animals of these strange new lands.

The young Charles Darwin was one such naturalist on a survey voyage of the English vessel *H.M.S. Beagle* to South America, beginning in 1831. On this voyage, Darwin began to formulate his ideas concerning the theory of evolution. Another of the great voyages of exploration in the study of the ocean biome was the expedition of *H.M.S. Challenger* in 1872. This voyage was conducted specifically to explore and chart the oceans, and collect and describe marine organisms. Some of the famous museums and universities in England still have preserved specimens of animals, plants, and bottom sediments collected on the *Challenger* expedition.

The most rapid growth in our knowledge of the oceans has come in the 20th century. Technology has aided the accumulation of knowledge. Sonar, or echo sounding, developed in the 1920s, enabled scientists to map the floor of the ocean in detail. The development of airplanes and aerial photography allowed people to accurately map coastlines.

Probably one of the most useful tools for the exploration of the sea is the technology to enable people to descend underwater to observe the ocean world firsthand. During the early 1800s, the use of "hardhats" was developed. Hardhat divers wore heavy helmets and suits and were lowered into the sea on cables. They were dependent upon pumps on the surface to pump air down to them. This "helmet and hose" technology allowed people to explore and work underwater, but with a restricted range of mobility. In 1943, the Frenchmen

The development of SCUBA has greatly aided the exploration and use of the oceans. This diver is planting seagrass as part of a habitat restoration project.

Jacques-Yves Cousteau and Emile Gagnan perfected the aqualung or SCUBA. For the first time, aided by mask, fins, and SCUBA, people could swim through the underwater environment with the freedom of a fish.

The use of the diving bell, or bathysphere, permitted people to descend much deeper into the ocean than they could with SCUBA or hardhats. The air in the bell is kept at the same pressure as at the surface. Thick walls of steel or aluminum resist the tremendous pressures of the deep ocean. Early diving bells were lowered by cables from ships. In 1934 William Beebe, a naturalist, and Otis Bartin, the designer of the diving bell, were lowered to a depth of 3,028 feet (918 meters) off Bermuda. For the first time, people viewed the deep oceans with their own eyes.

In the 1950s, the Swiss engineer Auguste Piccard developed the bathyscaph, a steel ball suspended from a large gasoline-filled float, with iron pellets for weight. Gasoline is lighter than water, but is not compressed as air would be, and because of this, the gasoline provides flotation. Like a hot-air balloon in the atmosphere, the bathyscaph permitted people to descend and ascend to and from the deep ocean without having to depend on an attachment to the surface. Deep-diving subs developed within the last twenty years are even more advanced. They have propellers or special jets, powered by electric motors, that enable them to move about freely and explore the deep oceans. They have external robotic arms which let them gather samples from the bottom.

Most recently, people have begun to live under the ocean to study and work in it. Cousteau pioneered some early experiments in living undersea. In the early 1960s, his CONSHELF projects experimented with undersea habitation. During this same time, the United States Navy was experimenting with living undersea in the SEALAB projects. Today, commercial divers working on open ocean oil drilling platforms use equipment and techniques developed in these early projects.

OUR USE OF THE OCEAN RESOURCES

The oceans of the world contain immense amounts of natural resources; minerals, oil, and food. People have always used these resources, and they have used the seas to transport goods and themselves. The sea is also a source of recreation and pleasure for many people.

Food

The main groups of animals used for food by people are fish and "shellfish," or invertebrates, of which shrimp, crabs, lobster, clams, and oysters are examples. Fish and shellfish are caught for food using many methods, but the most common methods use some type of net. Crabs and lobsters are caught with traps. People catch fish for fun using fishing rods and reels.

The large marine animals are also used for food. Sea turtles are caught by hand or with nets and used as food by native peoples and sailors in some parts of the world. Whales are usually caught by harpooning the animal and then killing it. Today, few countries of the world rely on whaling or sea turtles for much of their seafood. Unfortunately, overharvest of these animals has seriously reduced their numbers in the oceans.

It is only recently that people have learned that the food resources of the oceans are not limitless. We now know that catching too many individuals of a species of fish or other animal can seriously reduce the populations of that species. This can be caused by overharvest of adults in offshore waters or by catching too many young fish in coastal areas. Many coastal states in the United States have laws designating specific seasons of the year when certain species of fish may or may not be caught, and specifying that only certain sizes of fish may be taken. These laws are set up so that adult fish can produce young and so the young fish can grow to maturity before being caught and used for food.

Oil and Minerals

Beneath the oceans lie vast quantities of oil and minerals. The oil resources underneath the sea are already being tapped. Drilling platforms in the Gulf of Mexico, the North Sea, and other areas explore for and extract the oil reserves laying deep beneath the floor of the ocean.

Oil is a nonrenewable source of energy. When all of the oil present in the earth's crust is used up there will be no more for millions more years. Some people argue that we must explore for and tap the oil reserves under the sea until we develop other sources of energy to take the place of oil. Other people believe that the risk of the environmental damage that may result from an oil spill is too great to allow offshore drilling to take place. Offshore drilling is a very controversial topic because of these two opposing views.

The sea also holds vast amounts of minerals; iron, copper, manganese, nickel, and other metals are found on the floor of the ocean. The technology to harvest these minerals is just beginning to be developed. At the same time, our incomplete knowledge of the ecology of the deep ocean communities means that we have to pursue undersea mineral harvest carefully until we have a better understanding of what effects our mining activities may have on the creatures of the deep sea.

Transportation

People use the sea to economically transport large amounts of goods and materials and to transport themselves. Large freighters and tankers carry fertilizer, grain, machinery, automobiles, and liquid cargos between countries. Until the development of economical air travel, travel by ship was the only way persons could travel from one continent to another.

Many of the coastal cities of the world are located near large ports that handle this commercial shipping. Shipping ports are usually located in bays or estuaries. Most ports originally began in these areas because they offered shelter from storms. Bays and estuaries often have shallow depths, so channels have been dredged to allow large ships to enter. Dredging and water pollution from large ports have created many stresses on the natural communities of the estuary or bay.

POLLUTION AND HABITAT DESTRUCTION

The animals and plants living in the ocean are influenced by physical conditions such as salinity, temperature, and tides, and by biological conditions such as predation and competition. People can also influence the animals and plants of the ocean. The most serious threats to the ocean biome today are the effects of humans on the ocean by pollution and by the destruction of ocean habitat.

Water Pollution

There are two main types of water pollution: point source pollution and nonpoint source pollution.

Point source pollution is pollution coming from a source that can be easily identified. A discharge pipe dumping chemicals from a

Industrial development may have harmful effects on the marine environment. The natural environment must be considered in the development of ports and other large-scale water front development.

factory into the ocean is point source pollution. Pollution from point sources can take several forms; it can be chemical products (such as toxic metals, pesticides, or other chemicals), it can be excessive nutrients (such as discharge from a sewage treatment plant), or it can be thermal pollution (discharge of hot water from a power plant or other factory). All of these types of pollutants can have harmful effects on marine organisms.

An increase in public awareness of the harmful effects of pollution in the 1960s and 1970s resulted in the passage of numerous laws in the United States restricting point source discharges to ocean waters. These

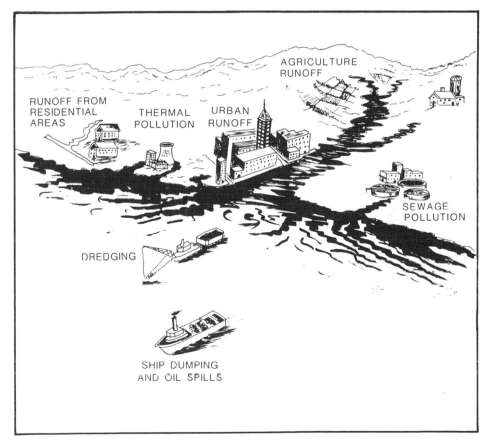

This drawing shows some of the major sources of water pollution in the ocean.

laws have, in some areas, improved the water quality of polluted areas due to a decrease in the amount of pollution being dumped into the water.

A second source of water pollution problems is non-point source pollution. This is pollution that comes from a source that is difficult to identify. Rain that falls on streets and sidewalks is drained into storm sewers that dump into coastal waters. This stormwater runoff is nonpoint pollution. The runoff contains dirt, oil, nutrients, grease, and other chemicals which pollute the ocean. Runoff from farms may also cause pollution, since it may contain sediment, pesticides, or nutrients. Nonpoint pollution in the form of runoff from urban or agricultural areas is currently one of the biggest water pollution problems in the United States.

A third type of water pollution problem, which can't be classified as point or nonpoint source pollution, is ocean dumping. For many years, people have used the oceans as a gigantic garbage can, dumping their refuse and waste into the sea. Along many coastlines, aluminum cans, bottles, wood, styrofoam, old tires, and other trash are regularly washed ashore.

In the summer of 1988, Americans were horrified to read stories of medical waste (needles, syringes, and assorted hospital garbage) washing up onto their public beaches. This was a dramatic example of what is actually fairly common along our coastlines, and it represents a serious threat to the health of the oceans.

Habitat Destruction

The destruction of habitats that are important to marine organisms is as harmful to the oceans as pollution of the water. The coast is a beautiful and desirable place to live. As more people have moved to live near the ocean, the high prices commanded by waterfront land has given rise to the practice of dredging and filling to create this land.

Many acres of valuable marine habitat have been lost to dredge and fill along the coast, including coastal marshes, swamps and grassbeds. These habitats serve as nurseries for the young of many species of fish and shellfish caught by people for food. Declines in catches of many species of fish have been shown to be directly due to destruction of this nursery habitat.

CONSERVATION

As people have become aware of how they can affect the ocean, they have become concerned about damage to the ocean and its inhabitants. This concern has been expressed in many valuable ways. Organizations such as the International Oceanographic Foundation and the American Littoral Society have encouraged governments to pass laws protecting the oceans. Laws have been passed in many countries that regulate the discharge of pollutants to coastal waters. In the United States, there are laws in many coastal states that now protect salt marsh and seagrass habitats from dredging and filling. In some states, attempts are being made to restore coastal habitat by actually replanting salt marshes and seagrass beds.

Many rare species of marine animals are now protected by laws. The United States does not allow the importation of any product made with the shells of sea turtles, since the survival of many of these animals are endangered. Every country in the world but two (Japan and the Soviet Union) have discontinued the practice of commercial whaling, due to the small number of many species of whales remaining in the oceans.

Many countries are beginning to study seriously the use of aquaculture to produce seafood. Aquaculture is the science of raising and harvesting certain species of marine life specifically for food. Japan relies very much on aquaculture to produce food and other marine products. Oysters and seaweeds are grown for food on racks floating in bays and harbors. Shrimp are hatched in special hatcheries, then moved to outdoor pools to grow.

Two of the most important conditions needed to insure the survival of the world's oceans are:

Knowledge

It is extremely important to continue to study and research the oceans of the world. We must have a thorough understanding of how the marine communities of animals and plants are organized and the environmental conditions (physical and biological) that create that organization in order to evaluate the effects of human activities on those communities.

Public Concern

All people have to care about the oceans. It is the concern and activity of caring people that have resulted in improvements and benefits to the oceans. If people do not care about becoming informed about environmental problems affecting the oceans, and if they do not convey to their government their concern, then our children or our grandchildren will inherit very serious problems.

All persons can help with the efforts to protect and preserve the world's oceans. Possibly, you may do this by choosing a career in the study or protection of the ocean's resources. Most importantly, you can help by being a concerned and informed citizen. Read newspapers, magazines, and books to keep informed about problems affecting the oceans and express your concern about these problems to your government.

Glossary

abyssal plain—the flat, level portions of the deep ocean floor found at depths of 6,600 to 9,900 feet (2,000 to 3,000 meters).

aerobic environments—areas with adequate oxygen to support life.

anaerobic environments—areas without adequate oxygen to support life.

aquaculture—the science of growing and harvesting aquatic plants and animals specifically for consumption by people.

aqualung—A device that permits people to descend underwater and move about freely, carrying a supply of air with them in a tank worn on the back. Most aqualungs consist of an air tank and a demand regulator, which feeds air to the diver.

autotrophic—refers to the ability of a living organism to produce its own food from simple elements.

barrier island—a coastal island separated from the mainland by a lagoon.

benthic—refers to organisms that live on or within the bottom of the ocean.

biome—an ecosystem; the community of living organisms found within a physical habitat. There are marine or oceanic biomes, freshwater biomes, and terrestrial biomes.

byssus—the clump of threads manufactured by species of mussels and some other types of bivalves which they use to anchor themselves.

continental shelf—the rim or shelf of land surrounding the continents of the world. The shelf is a part of the continent. Depth of the shelf varies from 0 to 660 feet (0 to 200 meters).

continental slope—the steep dropoff from the continental shelf to the abyssal plains and other features of the deep ocean bottom.

copepod—microscopic, planktonic crustaceans found in all of the world's major oceans and in freshwater biomes.

coral reef—the underwater structures produced by the action of coral colonies, which extract calcium carbonate from seawater to form the reefs.

current—the horizontal movement of masses of water. Examples include the major ocean currents, tidal currents, and longshore currents.

decomposers—organisms such as bacteria and fungi that break down dead animals and plants.

detritus—particles of dead and decaying animal and plant material.

diatom—types of microscopic phytoplankton plants found in oceans and freshwater biomes throughout the world. Usually they are most abundant in temperate waters. They are characterized by a cell wall composed of silica.

dinoflagellate—types of microscopic phytoplankton plants found in oceans throughout the world. Usually they are most abundant in subtropical and tropical seas. They are characterized by the presence of flagella.

epibenthic—refers to organisms that live on the surface of the bottom (such as a rock surface).

estuary—an area along the coast where freshwater enters (from a river, creek or spring) and mixes with seawater.

eutrophic areas—water locations that have an overabundance of plant nutrients, either naturally or due to pollution.

habitat—the specific place where an organism prefers to live, and where it feeds and raises its young.

herbivore—an animal that feeds on plants.

infauna—animals that live within the sediment, sometimes within burrows or tubes.

inlet—the connection between a bay or lagoon and the open ocean; also called a pass.

intertidal zone—the area on the coast between the levels of high and low tide.

mangrove swamp—term given to the forests of mangrove trees found on low-energy subtropical and tropical coastlines.

mutualism—an association between different two kinds of organisms that is beneficial to both.

nekton—larger, free-swimming organisms found in the pelagic portion of the ocean and freshwater biomes.

nutrients—chemical substances required by plants and animals; examples are nitrates and phosphates.

oceanic ridges—the systems of underwater mountains found on the bottom of the deep oceans.

pelagic—refers to the water overlaying the bottom of ocean and freshwater biomes and the organisms that live within that water.

plankton—term given to the microscopic organisms and plants found in the pelagic portion of ocean and freshwater biomes.

pollution—term given to the introduction of waste products, chemicals, and other substances into the environment by humans.

salinity—refers to the total amount of salt present in seawater; measured in parts per thousand (‰).

salt marsh—the communities of grasses and rushes found in the intertidal zone on low-energy sandy, temperate shores.

sand dunes—the mounds of sand with their associated communities of animals and plants found on high-energy sandy coastlines.

seagrass bed—the communities of underwater grass-like plants found on low-energy, sandy coastlines in many coastal areas.

SEALAB—the undersea living experiments conducted by the United States Navy in the early 1960's.

seamount—an underwater mountain formed by volcanic activity.

silica—a glass-like mineral used by diatoms to construct their cell wall.

sodium chloride—the most common salt found in seawater; abbreviated chemically as NaCl.

splash zone—coastal areas above the high tide level which are wetted only by splashing from waves.

subtidal zone—coastal areas below the low tide level which are rarely exposed to the air.

symbiosis—a relationship between two organisms.

thermal rift vent community—the communities of animals found around thermal vents in the floor of the deep ocean.

thermocline—a zone of sudden temperature transition in a body of water between two depth layers.

tide—the periodic rise and fall of the level of the water each day caused by the gravitational pull of the moon and sun on the oceans of the world.

trench—deep areas on the floor of the ocean similar to underwater canyons. Depths of trenches are generally deeper than 19,800 feet (6,000 meters).

upwelling—the movement of masses of water up from the bottom of the ocean.

vertical migration—term which describes the daily movement of certain types of organisms deeper during the day and towards the surface at night.

warm-blooded animal—an animal that maintains a constant body temperature (no matter what the temperature of the environment is). Mammals and birds are the two types of warm-blooded animals.

wave—disturbance that travels through a medium such as water or air.

zooplankton—microscopic animals found in the oceans.

Further Reading

Abbot, R. Tucker. *Seashells of North America: A Guide to Field Identification*. New York: Golden Press, 1969.

Amos, W. H. *The Life of the Seashore*. New York: McGraw-Hill, 1966.

Berrill, N. J. *The Life of the Ocean*. New York: McGraw-Hill, 1966.

Carson, Rachel L. *The Edge of the Sea*. New York: Houghton-Mifflin, 1979.

Carson, Rachel L. *The Sea Around Us*. New York: Oxford University Press, 1989.

Cousteau, Jacques-Yves and Dumas, F. *The Silent World*. New York: Lyons and Burford, 1987.

Gosner, Kenneth. *A Field Guide to the Atlantic Seashore: Peterson Field Guide Series*. Boston: Houghton-Mifflin Co., 1982.

Meinkoth, Norman A. *The Audubon Society Field Guide to North American Seashore Creatures*. New York: Alfred A. Knopf, 1981.

Meyerson, A. Lee. *Seawater: A Delicate Balance*. Hillside, N.J.: Enslow Publishers, 1988.

Reed, Willow. *Succession: From Field to Forest*. Hillside, N.J.: Enslow Publishers, 1991.

Robison, B. H. *Lurkers of the Deep: Life Within the Ocean Depths*. New York: David McKay Co., Inc., 1978.

Sumich, J. L. *An Introduction to the Biology of Marine Life*. Dubuque, Iowa: William C. Brown Co. Publishers, 1987.

Teal, John M. and Mildred Teal. *Life and Death of a Salt Marsh*. New York: Ballantine, 1983.

Thorson, G. *Life in the Sea*. New York: McGraw-Hill, 1971.

Zim, Herbert S. and Lester Ingle. *Seashores: A Guide to Animals and Plants Along the Beaches*. New York: Golden Press, 1955.

Zim, Herbert S. and Hurst Shoemaker. *Fishes: A Guide to Fresh and Saltwater Species*. New York: Golden Press, 1987.

Index